D0948831

The
Emancipation
Proclamation

Other books in the At Issue in History series:

The Emancipation Proclamation

Maria L. Howell, *Book Editor*

Bruce Glassman, *Vice President*
Bonnie Szumski, *Publisher*
Helen Cothran, *Managing Editor*
Scott Barbour, *Series Editor*

 **OPPOSING VIEWPOINTS® SERIES** **AT ISSUE IN HISTORY**

GREENHAVEN PRESS
An imprint of Thomson Gale, a part of The Thomson Corporation

THOMSON
—✳—
GALE

Detroit • New York • San Francisco • San Diego • New Haven, Conn.
Waterville, Maine • London • Munich

LIBRARY OF CONGRESS CATALOGING-IN-PUBLICATION DATA

The Emancipation Proclamation / Maria L. Howell, book editor.
    p. cm. — (At issue in history)
Includes bibliographical references and index.
ISBN 0-7377-2276-2 (lib. : alk. paper)
    1. United States. President (1861–1865 : Lincoln). Emancipation Proclamation.
2. Slaves—Emancipation—United States. 3. Slaves—Emancipation—United States—Sources. I. Howell, Maria L. II. Series.
E453.E427 2006
973.7'14—dc22   2005046341

Contents

Chapter 3: Historical Assessment of the Emancipation Proclamation

Foreword

Historian Robert Weiss defines history simply as "a record and interpretation of past events." Both elements—record and interpretation—are necessary, Weiss argues.

> Names, dates, places, and events are the essence of history. But historical writing is not a compendium of facts. It consists of facts placed in a sequence to tell a connected story. A work of history is not merely a story, however. It also must analyze what happened and *why*—that is, it must interpret the past for the reader.

For example, the events of December 7, 1941, that led President Franklin D. Roosevelt to call it "a date which will live in infamy" are fairly well known and straightforward. A force of Japanese planes and submarines launched a torpedo and bombing attack on American military targets in Pearl Harbor, Hawaii. The surprise assault sank five battleships, disabled or sank fourteen additional ships, and left almost twenty-four hundred American soldiers and sailors dead. On the following day, the United States formally entered World War II when Congress declared war on Japan.

These facts and consequences were almost immediately communicated to the American people who heard reports about Pearl Harbor and President Roosevelt's response on the radio. All realized that this was an important and pivotal event in American and world history. Yet the news from Pearl Harbor raised many unanswered questions. Why did Japan decide to launch such an offensive? Why were the attackers so successful in catching America by surprise? What did the attack reveal about the two nations, their people, and their leadership? What were its causes, and what were its effects? Political leaders, academic historians, and students look to learn the basic facts of historical events and to read the intepretations of these events by many different sources, both primary and secondary, in order to develop a more complete picture of the event in a historical context.

In the case of Pearl Harbor, several important questions surrounding the event remain in dispute, most notably the role of President Roosevelt. Some historians have blamed his policies for deliberately provoking Japan to attack in order to propel America into World War II; a few have gone so far as to accuse him of knowing of the impending attack but not informing others. Other historians, examining the same event, have exonerated the president of such charges, arguing that the historical evidence does not support such a theory.

The Greenhaven At Issue in History series recognizes that many important historical events have been interpreted differently and in some cases remain shrouded in controversy. Each volume features a collection of articles that focus on a topic that has sparked controversy among eyewitnesses, contemporary observers, and historians. An introductory essay sets the stage for each topic by presenting background and context. Several chapters then examine different facets of the subject at hand with readings chosen for their diversity of opinion. Each selection is preceded by a summary of the author's main points and conclusions. A bibliography is included for those students interested in pursuing further research. An annotated table of contents and thorough index help readers to quickly locate material of interest. Taken together, the contents of each of the volumes in the Greenhaven At Issue in History series will help students become more discriminating and thoughtful readers of history.

Introduction

In the history of the United States, no issue has been more contentious than slavery. Central to the debate was a discrepancy that dated from early in America's founding and was cemented at the writing of America's constitution. The nation was founded on a document that both guaranteed liberty, equality, and justice for all, and condoned slavery for its black citizens. This contradiction fueled the debate on slavery: Slaveholding states of the South believed their position was constitutionally protected and framed any attempt to limit slavery as an attack on states' rights. Northern states, on the other hand, argued that slavery gave the South an unfair economic advantage because of black free labor. In addition, a minority of very vocal abolitionist groups worked to try to abolish slavery. As the United States grew, and interests between the North and South continued to diverge, every political decision made in Congress seemed to revolve around keeping the two sides appeased. Eventually, the issue of slavery could not be resolved in the courts. It could only be resolved by war, and it would fall to Abraham Lincoln, as president, to find a way to preserve a union where two opposing societies, an agrarian South based on slave labor, and an increasingly industrialized North that had no such legacy, were essentially at odds.

By the time of Lincoln's bid for the presidency, the future of the United States clearly rested on resolving the slavery issue. It is important to remember that only a few white Northerners (and a handful of white Southerners) considered themselves abolitionists, even by 1861, and the vast majority of whites in both the South and North harbored racist views about blacks. Nevertheless, slavery had both economic and political ramifications that would make the North mobilize against it.

The Civil War did not break out because the North decided that the time had come to abolish slavery by force if necessary. Despite a crescendo of abolitionist exposés of slavery as a horrific institution, what moved Northern opinion decisively against slavery was fear that slave owners and their supporters were gaining control of the federal government and were preparing to seize control of the West, excluding free white farmers and laborers who could not compete with slave labor.

For Southerners, slavery boiled down to a states' rights issue rather than than a moral issue. The idea of states' rights was particularly important as new territories opened up in the West and the expansion of slavery into these territories became an increasingly enticing proposition. The fight between North and South over the new territories continued to inflame the slavery debate and heightened tension between the opposing sides.

Lincoln's election to the presidency in 1860 dismayed Southerners and, surprisingly, many Northerners as well. Lincoln was not even on the ballot in the South—candidates did not have to appear on the ballot in every state—and so most Southerners felt completely disenfranchised. The South thought it had no choice but to secede from the Union. Alarmed Northerners believed Lincoln to be a radical abolitionist (which he was not), and feared that his election would empower blacks and lead to a race war in the South.

Before his election, Lincoln could see valid points on both sides—although personally opposed to slavery (though he did not consider blacks equal to whites), he also understood that slavery was a legal institution protected by the Constitution. Lincoln wanted to stop the spread of slavery to the new territories, but continue to allow it in the states where it was currently legal. However, with the passage of the Kansas-Nebraska Act in 1854, Lincoln grew more pessimistic about the country's ability to resolve the issue. By allowing slavery beyond the area originally agreed upon in the Missouri Compromise, the act virtually guaranteed continued violent disagreement about whether states should enter the union free or slave. Lincoln's opposition to the passage of the Kansas-Nebraska Act also made the slave-holding South believe that a union with Lincoln at its head could not be tolerated.

When war broke out, President Lincoln declared that his paramount intention was to save the union, not to free the slaves. Only when it became apparent that the Confederacy was not going to be quickly defeated on the battlefield did Lincoln decide to strike at the South by undermining

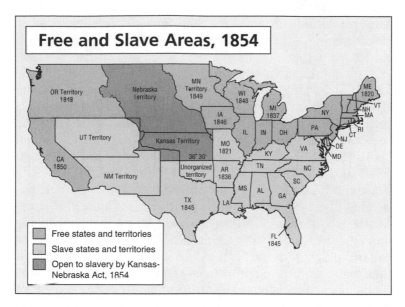

slavery. Lincoln issued a preliminary proclamation on September 22, 1862, stating that all slaves held in rebel states would be set free effective January 1, 1863. On that date, Lincoln issued his final Emancipation Proclamation, which declared that "all persons held as slaves" in rebel territories "are, and henceforward shall be free."

The Emancipation Proclamation signaled to Americans, and, indeed, to the whole world, that America's war objectives had changed. America would no longer tolerate the uneasy truce between the South and the North. Lincoln had officially declared war on slavery. When the war was over, the Union would finally adhere to the promise of "equality for all."

News that they would be emancipated if the Union won spread quickly among the Confederacy's slaves, but most in the Deep South did not leave their white owners. Only as Union troops roundly defeated a particular area did its slaves abandon their work and follow Union troops in droves.

While the proclamation, therefore, had a minimal impact on slaves in the Deep South, by enabling freed slaves to enlist in the Union army, it gave blacks the opportunity to fight for their own freedom. About 186,000 black men served in the Union army, constituting one-tenth of all Union soldiers.

So slavery died as a result of slave owners' decision to

leave the Union and fight for Southern independence, a decision made not in response to abolitionists' determination to destroy slavery on moral grounds, but because political and economic divisions forged an enormous gap in the Union that could not be breached or endured. After the slave owners' rebellion was quelled on the battlefield and their slaves were declared freed, the Union states ratified the Thirteenth Amendment to the Constitution, which abolished slavery everywhere in the new United States. In 1868 and 1870, respectively, two new amendments, the Fourteenth and Fifteenth, promised former slaves their basic civil liberties, including the right (of black men) to vote. But it would take almost a century, until the civil rights movement of the 1950s through the early 1970s, before legal and political obstacles to African Americans' exercise of their hard-won freedom were overthrown. Yet still the subtle barriers of racism and exclusion, legacies of centuries of American slavery, remain to haunt the land.

Chapter 1

Before the Emancipation Proclamation

1

Owning Slaves
Is a Legal Right

Robert Barnwell Rhett

With the election of President Lincoln in 1860, slaveholding states in the South believed that the end of slavery was inevitable. The first state to secede from the Union was South Carolina. In an address given on the day South Carolina seceded from the Union, excerpted below, Robert Barnwell Rhett denounces the U.S. government for violating the constitutional rights of slaveholders to own slaves. Rhett served as a U.S. representative from 1837 to 1849, and as a U.S. senator from 1850 to 1852. He was also known as one of the most strident "fire-eaters," who were staunch defenders of slavery and advocates for secession. In his speech, Rhett maintains that the republic, established by the Constitution, is a republic that includes slaveholding states. He argues that the growth of antislavery fervor and the election of President Lincoln leaves South Carolina no choice but to secede from the Union.

The one great evil from which all other evils have flowed, is the overthrow of the Constitution of the United States. The Government of the United States is no longer the government of a confederate republic, but of a consolidated democracy. It is no longer a free government, but a despotism. It is, in fact, such a government as Great Britain attempted to set over our fathers, and which was resisted and defeated by a seven years struggle for independence. . . .

No man can for a moment believe that our ancestors in-

Robert Barnwell Rhett, "Address to the People of South Carolina, Assembled in Convention, to the People of Slaveholding States of the United States," in *The Political History of the United States During the Great Rebellion*, by Edward McPherson. Washington, DC: Philip & Solomons, 1864.

tended to establish over their posterity exactly the same sort of Government they had overthrown. The great object of the Constitution of the United States, in its internal operation, was, doubtless, to secure the great end of the Revolution—a limited free Government—a Government limited to those matters only which were general and common to all portions of the United States. All sectional or local interests were to be left to the States. By no other arrangement would they obtain free government by a Constitution common to so vast a Confederacy. Yet, by gradual and steady encroachments on the part of the North, and submission on the part of the South, the limitations in the Constitution have been swept away, and the Government of the United States has become consolidated, with a claim of limitless powers in its operations. . . .

No man can for a moment believe that our ancestors intended to establish over their posterity exactly the same sort of Government they had overthrown.

It cannot be believed that our ancestors would have assented to any union whatever with the people of the North if the feelings and opinions now existing among them had existed when the Constitution was framed. There was then no tariff—no negro fanaticism. It was the delegates from New England who proposed in the Convention which framed the Constitution, to the delegates from South Carolina and Georgia, that if they would agree to give Congress the power of regulating commerce by a majority, that they would support the extension of the African slave-trade for twenty years. African Slavery existed in all the States but one. The idea that they would be made to pay that tribute to their Northern confederates which they had refused to pay to Great Britain, or that the institution of African Slavery would be made the grand basis of a sectional organization of the North to rule the South, never crossed their imaginations. The Union of the Constitution was a Union of slaveholding States. It rests on Slavery, by prescribing a representation in Congress for three-fifths of our slaves. There is nothing in the proceedings of the Convention which framed the Constitution to show that the Southern States would have formed any other union; and still less that they would have formed a union with more powerful non-slaveholding States, having a majority in both branches of the Legislature of the Government. They were guilty of no such folly. Time and the progress of things have totally altered the relations between the Northern and Southern States since the Union was first established. That identity of feeling, interests, and institutions which once existed is gone. They are now divided between agricultural and manufacturing and commercial States—between slaveholding and non-slaveholding States. Their institutions and industrial pursuits have made them totally different peoples. That equality in the Government between the two sections of the Union which once existed, no longer exists. We but imitate the policy of our fathers in dissolving a union with non-slaveholding confederates, and seeking a confederation with slave-holding States.

The people of the North have not left us in doubt as to their designs and policy.

Experience has proved that slave-holding States can not be safe in subjection to non-slaveholding States. Indeed, no people ever expect to preserve their rights and liberties unless they are in their own custody. To plunder and oppress where plunder and oppression can be practiced with impunity, seems to be the natural order of things. The fairest portions of the world have been turned into wildernesses, and the most civilized and prosperous communities have been impoverished and ruined by Anti-Slavery fanaticism. The people of the North have not left us in doubt as to their designs and policy. United as a section in the late Presidential election, they have elected as the exponent of their policy one who has openly declared that all the States of the United States must be made Free States or Slave States. It is true that among those who aided in this election, there are various shades of Anti-Slavery hostility. But if African Slavery in the Southern States be the evil their political combinations affirm it to be, the requisitions of an inexorable logic must lead them to emancipation. If it is right to preclude or abolish Slavery in a territory, why should it be allowed to remain in the States? The one is not at all more unconstitutional than the other, according to the decisions of the Supreme Court of the United States. And when it is considered that the Northern States will soon have the power to make that Court what they please, and that the Constitution has never been any barrier whatever to their exercise of power, what check can there be in the unrestrained councils of the North to emancipation? There is sympathy in association, which carries men along without principle; but when there is principle, and that principle is fortified by long existing prejudices and feelings, association is omnipotent in party influences. In spite of all disclaimers and professions there can be but one end to the submission by the South to the rule of a sectional Anti-Slavery Government at Washington; and that end, directly or indirectly, must be the emancipation of the slaves of the South. The hypocrisy of thirty years—the faithlessness of their whole course from the commencement of our union with them— show that the people of the non-slaveholding North are not and cannot be safe associates of the slaveholding South under a common Government. Not only their fanaticism, but their erroneous views of the principles of free governments, render it doubtful whether, separated from the South, they can maintain a free Government among themselves. Brute numbers with them is the great element of free Government. A majority is infallible and omnipotent. "The right divine to rule in kings" is only transferred to their majority.

To Restrain the Majority

The very object of all constitutions, in free, popular Governments, is to restrain the majority. Constitutions, therefore, according to their theory, must be most unrighteous inventions, restricting liberty. None ought to exist, but the body politic ought simply to have a political organization, to bring out and enforce the will of a majority. This theory may be harmless in a small community, having an identity of interests and pursuits, but over a vast State—still more, over a vast Confederacy, having various and conflicting interests and pursuits—it is a remorseless despotism. In resisting it, as applicable to ourselves, we are vindicating the great cause of free government, more important, perhaps, to the world than the existence of the United States. Nor in resisting it, do we intend to depart from the safe instrumentality the system of government we have established with them requires. In separating from them we invade no rights—no interest of theirs. We violate no obligation of duty to them. As separate, independent States in Convention, we made the Constitution of the United States with them; and as separate, independent States, each State acting for itself, we adopted it. South Carolina, acting in her sovereign capacity, now thinks [it] proper to secede from the Union. She did not part with her sovereignty in adopting the Constitution. The last thing a State can be presumed to have surrendered is her sovereignty. Her sovereignty is her life. Nothing but a clear, express grant, can alienate it. Inference should be dumb. Yet it is not at all surprising that those who have construed away all the limitations of the Constitution, should also by construction claim the annihilation of the sovereignty of the States. Having abolished all barriers to their omnipotence by their faithless constructions in the operations of the General Government, it is most natural that they should endeavor to do the same toward us in the States. The truth is, they having violated the express provisions of the Constitution, it is at an end as a compact. It is morally obligatory only on those who choose to accept its perverted terms. South Carolina, deeming the compact not only violated in particular features, but virtually abolished by her Northern confederates, withdraws herself as a party from its obligations. The right to do so is denied by her Northern confederates. They desire to establish a despotism, not only omnipotent in Congress, but omnipotent over the States; and as if to manifest the imperious necessity of our secession, they threaten us with the sword, to coerce submission to their rule.

2

The Abolition of Slavery Should Be an Objective of the Civil War

George W. Julian

The radical faction of Lincoln's own party, known as the Radical Republicans, were the foremost advocates of the immediate destruction of slavery. Before the Civil War they remained steadfast in their belief that slavery was morally wrong and were adamant that slavery not spread to the territories. During the Civil War and before the Emancipation Proclamation, the Radical Republicans wanted the full force of the Union army brought to bear against rebel forces in the effort to destroy slavery. Notable among those who favored making emancipation the primary objective of the war was George W. Julian, a Republican from Indiana's Fifth District. In a Congressional speech, "The Cause and Cure of our National Troubles," given on the state of the Union, on January 14, 1862, and excerpted below, Julian vehemently argues that it is imperative and essential that Union forces destroy slavery since this would in effect weaken and demoralize rebel forces and undermine their capacity to withstand Union forces. Julian's fiery rhetoric not only had the power to enflame antislavery sentiments in a time of war, his utterances provide a window into the soul of a nation wrestling with the moral issues of human bondage.

Mr. Chairman, our *power* to destroy slavery now, I believe, is not questioned. The law of nations applicable to a state of war takes from this rebel power every constitu-

George W. Julian, *The Cause and Cure of Our National Troubles, Speeches on Political Questions*. Westport, CT: Negro Universities Press, 1970.

19

tional refuge it could claim in a time of peace. The principle is thus declared by the illustrious statesman [John
Quincy Adams] whose authority I have already quoted re-
specting another topic:—

> I lay this down as the law of nations. I say that the mil-
> itary authority takes, for the time, the place of all mu-
> nicipal institutions, slavery among the rest. Under that
> state of things, so far from its being true that the States
> where slavery exists have the exclusive management of
> the subject, not only the President of the United
> States, but the Commander of the army, has power to
> order the universal emancipation of the slaves.

And again:—

> From the instant that your slaveholding States become
> the theatre of war, civil, servile, or foreign, from that
> instant the war powers of Congress extend to interfer-
> ence with the institution of slavery, in every way in
> which it can be interfered with, from a claim of indem-
> nity for slaves taken or destroyed, to the cession of a
> State burdened with slavery to a foreign power.

This, Sir, is the grand weapon which the rebels have
placed in our hands, and we should use it as a matter of clear
and unhesitating duty. Not that the Constitution is so ab-
solutely perfect, or so entirely sacred, that we can in no
event disregard it. The nation is greater than the Constitution, because it made the Constitution. We had a country
before we had a Constitution, and at all hazards we must
save it. The Constitution was made for the people, not the
people for the Constitution. Cases may arise in which patriotism itself may demand that we trample under our feet
some of the most vital principles of the Constitution, under
the exigencies of war. "Man is more than constitutions; better rot beneath the sod, Than be true to Church and State,
while we are doubly false to God."

But so far as emancipation is concerned, constitutional
difficulties, if any existed, are no longer in the way, since the
Constitution itself recognizes the war power of the government, which the rebels have compelled us to employ against
them. They have sown the wind, now let them reap the
whirlwind. We have leave to do what the great body of the
people have hitherto excused themselves from doing, on the

ground of impassable constitutional barriers, and our failure to act will be as criminal as the blessings of universal freedom would be priceless. "Man's liberty is God's opportunity." Not for all the wealth or honors of the universe should we now withhold our suffrage from the proposition to "proclaim liberty throughout all the land, to all the inhabitants thereof." Never, perhaps, in the history of any nation has so grand an occasion presented itself for serving the interests of humanity and freedom. And our responsibility, commensurate with our power, cannot be evaded. As we are freed from all antecedent obligations, we should deal with this remorseless oligarchy as if we were now at the beginning of the nation's life, and about to lay the foundations of empire in these States for ages to come. Our failure to give freedom to four millions of slaves would be a crime only to be measured by that of putting them in chains if they were free. If we could fully grasp this idea, our duty would become at once plain and imperative. We want not simply the military power to crush the rebellion, but the statesmanship that shall comprehend the crisis, and coin this "golden moment" into jewels of liberty and peace, for the future glory of the Republic.

Our failure to give freedom to four millions of slaves would be a crime only to be measured by that of putting them in chains if they were free.

Slavery, as I have already shown, has been the evil genius of the government from its birth. It has frustrated the design of our fathers to form "a more perfect Union." It has made it impossible to "establish justice," or "to secure domestic tranquillity." It has weakened the "common defense" by inviting foreign attack. It has opposed the "general welfare" by its merciless aristocracy in human flesh. It has denied us "the blessings of liberty," and given us its own innumerable curses instead. It has laid waste the fairest and most fertile half of the Republic, staying its progress in population, wealth, power, knowledge, civilization, the arts, and religion, thus heaping its burdens upon the whole nation, and costing us far more than the market value of all the millions in bonds. It has made the establishment of free schools and a general system of education impossible. It has branded labor as dishonorable and degrading. It has filled the ranks of infidelity, and brought religion itself into scorn, by bribing its professors to espouse its revolting iniquity. It has laid its wizard hand upon the mightiest statesmen and most royal intellects of the land, and harnessed them, like beasts of burden, in its loathsome service. It has denounced the Declaration of Independence as a political abomination, and dealt with our fathers as hypocrites, who affirmed its self-evident truths with a mental reservation, while appealing to the Supreme Judge of the world for the rectitude of their intentions. While spreading licentiousness, concubinage, and crime where it rules, it has lifted up its rebel voice in the name of the United States, in pleading the cause of despotism in every part of the civilized world. And, as the fitting climax of its career of lawlessness, it has aimed its dagger at the government that has fostered and guarded its life, and borne with its evil deeds, for more than seventy years. Sir, this mighty rebel against all law, human and divine, is now within our grasp, and we should strangle it forever. "New occasions teach new duties," and we should employ every weapon which the laws of war place within our reach in scourging it out of life. Not to do so, I repeat, would be the most heaven-daring recreancy to the grand trust which the circumstances of the hour have committed to our hands. God forbid that we should throw away this sublime occasion for serving his cause on earth, leaving our children to deplore our failure, as we to-day have to deplore the slighted opportunities of the past.

Slavery . . . has been the evil genius of the government from its birth. It has frustrated the design of our fathers to form "a more perfect Union."

Mr. Chairman, I have not referred, directly, to the question of humanity involved in the policy of crushing slavery by the war power. That subject has been considerably discussed before the country, and I do not propose to enter upon it here, beyond the incidental bearings of my argument. I waive none of my humanitarian grounds of opposition to slavery, but I prefer to deal with the practical issues of the crisis. I am for putting down slavery as a "military necessity," and as the dictate of the highest statesmanship. The immediate question before the country is the suppression of the rebellion, and the common laws which govern a war between nations apply to the conduct of a civil war. These laws are thus laid down by [Swiss philosopher Emierch de] Vattel:—

> Since the object of a just war is to repress injustice and violence, and forcibly to compel him who is deaf to the voice of justice, we have a right to put in practice against the enemy every measure that is necessary in order to weaken him, and disable him from resisting us and supporting his injustice; and we may choose such methods as are most efficacious, and best calculated to a attain the end in view, provided they be not of an odious kind, nor unjustifiable in themselves, and prohibited by the law of nature.

Sir, I insist upon the application of this well-recognized principle of public law. That the overthrow of slavery "is necessary in order to weaken" the enemy, "and disable him from resisting us and supporting his injustice," will not be disputed. That it would be a measure "most efficacious and best calculated to attain the end in view," is equally clear. Nor would it be "odious" to restore four millions of slaves to their natural rights, or "unjustifiable" in itself, or "prohibited by the law of nature." The friends of the Union need ask nothing more than the just application of the law of nations, and they certainly should be content with nothing less.

A right to subdue the rebels carries with it a right to employ the means of doing it, and of doing it effectively, and with the least possible cost. If slavery had not been made a party question, and trained us to yield an unnatural deference to its assumptions, we should have laid violent hands upon it at once. The thought of tenderly sparing it would not have occurred to any loyal man. As the most vulnerable point of the rebels, we should naturally have aimed at it our first and hardest blows; and I insist that we shall so far forget our party prejudices and the dread of "abolitionism," as to do what the dictates of common sense and a regard for our own safety so clearly demand. Facts, bloody and terrific, are every day proving that slavery, or the Republic, must perish. As the animating principle of the rebellion it stands between us and the Union, and we are compelled to smite it. To strike at it is to strike at treason; and to favor it in any way, however unwittingly, is to take sides with the rebels. They cherish it as the most precious of all earthly blessings. They love it with all the force of a long-fostered community of feeling; and the assertion is well attested, that the loss of a slave by Northern agency excites more sudden and widespread indignation than would the murder of his master. . . .

We want no war "conducted on peace principles." Every weapon within our reach must be grasped.

Mr. Chairman, the time has come for us to deal with the actual and stern facts of our condition. We must cease to regard the rebels as misguided men, whose infatuation is to be deplored, whilst we still hope to bring them to their senses. We must cease our attacks upon the strong points only of the enemy, whilst we fail to strike at the weak ones, and madly hope to woo them back to a sense of their folly and crime. We must abandon, entirely, the delusion that rebels and outlaws have any rights under the Constitution, and deal with them as rebels and outlaws. No men since the world was made were ever more in earnest. They hate us supremely. The rattlesnake is the fitly chosen symbol of their black confederacy. Their wrath is a desolating fire. The felt consciousness that they are in the wrong, and that we have for so many long years been the victims of their injustice, animates them with the fury of devils. They despise us all the more for every appeal we make to their sense of justice and fair play. They regard our free labor and free institutions with unutterable abhorrence. If they had the power they would exterminate us from the face of the earth. They have turned loose to prey upon the Republic the transmitted vices and diabolisms of two hundred years, and sooner than fail in their struggle they would light up heaven itself with the red glare of the Pit, and convert the earth into a carnival of devils. They have a mighty army, led by some of the ablest commanders in the world, and nerved for bloody deeds by all the power of desperation.

Sir, in such a contest we can spare no possible advantage.

We want no war "conducted on peace principles." Every weapon within our reach must be grasped. Every arrow in our quiver must be sped toward the heart of a rebel. Every obstacle in the path of our conquering hosts must be trodden down. War means ruin, destruction, death,—and loyal slaveholders, and loyal non-slaveholders must stand out of the way, in this tremendous encounter with the assassins of liberty and free government. All tenderness toward such a foe is treason to our cause, murder to our people, faithlessness to the grandest and holiest trust ever committed to a free people. The policy for which I plead, sooner or later, *must* be adopted, if the rebels are to be mastered, and every delay puts in peril the precious interests for which we fight. Let us act at once, putting forth all our power. Let the war be made just as terrific to the rebels as possible, consistently with the laws of war. This will be at once a work of mercy, and the surest means of our triumph. Let us not mock the Almighty by waiting till we are forced by needless calamities to do what should be done at once, as the dictate alike of humanity and policy; for it may happen, when this rebellion shall have hung crape on one hundred thousand doors in the free States, that a ruined country will taunt us with the victory which might have been ours, and leave us only the poor consolation of bitter and unavailing regrets.

3

Emancipating the Slaves Will Hasten the End of the Confederate Rebellion

Horace Greeley, with a reply by Abraham Lincoln

Horace Greeley was a *New York Tribune* editor and ardent supporter of the antislavery movement. In 1841 Greeley established the *New York Tribune*, which became well known throughout the United States. According to his biographies, many of his editorials on slavery may have been instrumental in shaping Northern attitudes toward slavery. In addition, his criticism of and support for U.S. presidents during his editorship earned him respect as a journalist. In this editorial, "The Prayer of Twenty Millions," Greeley reminds Lincoln of his duty as president to uphold the laws of United States. He demands that the president enforce the Confiscation Acts of 1861 and 1862 in border states, which permitted the seizure of Confederate property, including slaves, as a war measure. Thus far, Lincoln and his generals had refused to do so. Greeley therefore emphatically urges Lincoln to destroy slavery, since it is the "core and essence of this atrocious Rebellion" and as long as slavery existed, the rebellion would persist and continue. In one of his most famous letters, attached hereto, Lincoln replies to Greeley, articulating his desire to protect and preserve the Union at any cost.

Harold Holzer, ed., *Dear Mr. Lincoln: Letters to the President*. New York: Addison Wesley, 1993.

"The Prayer of Twenty Millions"

To Abraham Lincoln, President of the United States:
Dear Sir:—I do not intrude to tell you—for you must know already—that a great portion of those who triumphed in your election, and of all who desire the unqualified suppression of the Rebellion now desolating our country, are sorely disappointed and deeply pained by the policy you seem to be pursuing with regard to the slaves of Rebels. I write only to set succinctly and unmistakably before you what we require, what we think we have a right to expect, and of what we complain.

I. We require of you, as the first servant of the Republic, charged especially and pre-eminently with this duty, that you EXECUTE THE LAWS. Most emphatically do we demand that such laws as have been recently enacted, which therefore may fairly be presumed to embody the *present* will, and to be dictated by the *present* needs of the *Republic*, and which, after due consideration, have received your personal sanction, shall by you be carried into full effect, and that you publicly and decisively, instruct your subordinates that such laws exist, that they are binding on all functionaries and citizens, and that they are to be obeyed to the letter.

II. We think you are strangely and disastrously remiss in the discharge of your official and imperative duty with regard to the emancipating provisions of the new Confiscation Act. Those provisions were designed to fight Slavery with Liberty. They prescribe that men loyal to the Union, and willing to shed their blood in her behalf, shall no longer be held, with the nation's consent, in bondage to persistent, malignant traitors, who for twenty years have been plotting, and for sixteen months have been fighting to divide and destroy our country. Why these traitors should be treated with tenderness by you, to the prejudice of the dearest rights of loyal men, we cannot conceive.

III. We think you are unduly influenced by the counsels, the representations, the menaces, of certain fossil politicians hailing from the Border Slave States. Knowing well that the heartily, unconditionally loyal portion of the white citizens of those States, do not expect nor desire that slavery shall be upheld to the predjudice [sic] of the Union, (for the truth of which we appeal not only to every Republican residing in those States, but to such eminent loyalists as H. Winter

Davis, Parson Brownlow, the Union Central Committee of
Baltimore, and to the Nashville *Union*,) we ask you to consider that slavery is everywhere the inciting cause, and sus-
taining base of treason: the most slaveholding sections of
Maryland and Delaware being this day, though under the
Union flag, in full sympathy with the Rebellion, while the
free labor portions of Tennessee, and of Texas, though
writhing under the bloody heel of treason, are unconquer-
ably loyal to the Union. So emphatically is this the case, that
a most intelligent Union banker of Baltimore recently
avowed his confident belief that a majority of the present
Legislature of Maryland, though elected as and still profess-
ing to be Unionists, are at heart desirous of the triumph of
the Jeff. Davis conspiracy; and when asked how they could
be won back to loyalty, replied—"Only by the complete
Abolition of Slavery." It seems to us the most obvious truth,
that whatever strengthens or fortifies slavery in the Border
States strengthens also treason, and drives home the wedge
intended to divide the Union. Had you from the first refused
to recognize in those States, as here, any other than unconditional loyalty—that which stands for the Union, whatever
may become of slavery—those States would have been, and
would be, far more helpful and less troublesome to the defenders of the Union, than they have been, or now are.

---

*We complain that the Union cause has suffered,
and is now suffering immensely, from mistaken
deference to Rebel Slavery.*

IV. We think timid counsels in such a crisis calculated to
prove perilous, and probably disastrious [*sic*]. It is the duty
of a government as wantonly, wickedly assailed by Rebellion
as ours has been, to oppose force to force in a defiant,
dauntless spirit. It cannot afford to temporize with traitors
nor with semi-traitors. It must not bribe them to behave
themselves, nor make them fair promises in the hope of dis-
arming their causeless hostility. Representing a brave and
high-spirited people, it can afford to forfeit anything else
better than its own self-respect, or their admiring confi-
dence. For our Government even to seek, after war has been
made on it, to dispel the affected apprehensions of armed

traitors that their cherished privileges may be assailed by it, is to invite, insult and encourage hopes of its own downfall. The rush to arms of Ohio, Indiana, Illinois, is the true answer at once to the rebel raids of John Morgan [a Confederate cavalry raider], and the traitorous sophistries of Berrah Magoffin [the "neutral" Governor of Kentucky accused by unionists of being secretly pro-secession].

A Missed Opportunity

V. We complain that the Union cause has suffered, and is now suffering immensely, from mistaken deference to Rebel Slavery. Had you, Sir, in your Inaugural Address, unmistakably given notice that, in case the Rebellion already commenced were persisted in, and your efforts to preserve the Union and enforce the laws, should be resisted by armed force *you would recognize no loyal person as rightfully held in slavery by a traitor*, we believe the Rebellion would therein have received a staggering if not fatal blow. At that moment, according to the returns of the most recent elections, the Unionists were a large majority of the voters of the slave States. But they were composed in good part of the aged, the feeble, the wealthy, the timid—the young, the reckless, the aspiring, the adventurous, had already been largely lured by the gamblers and negro-traders, the politicians by trade and the conspirators by instinct, into the toils of treason. Had you then proclaimed that rebellion would strike the shackles from the slaves of every traitor, the wealthy and the cautious would have been supplied with a powerful inducement to remain loyal. As it was, every coward in the South soon became a traitor from fear; for loyalty was perilous, while treason seemed comparatively safe. Hence, the boasted unanimity of the South—a unanimity based on Rebel terrorism, and the fact that immunity and safety were found on that side, danger and probable death on ours. The Rebels from the first have been eager to confiscate, imprison, scourge and kill; we have fought wolves with the devices of sheep. The result is just what might have been expected. Tens of thousands are fighting in the Rebel ranks to-day whose original bias and natural leanings would have led them into ours.

VI. We complain that the Confiscation Act which you approved is habitually disregarded by your Generals, and that no word of rebuke for them from you has yet reached the public ear. Fremont's Proclamation and Hunter's Order favoring Emancipation were promptly annulled to you; while Halleck's No. 3, forbidding fugitives from slavery to Rebels to come within his lines—an order as unmilitary as inhuman, and which received the hearty approbation of every traitor in America—with scores of like tendency have never provoked even your remonstrance. We complain that the officers of your armies have habitually repelled, rather than invited the approach of slaves who would have gladly taken the risks of escaping from the Rebel masters to our camps, bringing intelligence often of inestimable value to the Union cause. We complain that those who have thus escaped to us, avowing a willingness to do for us whatever might be required, have been brutally and madly repulsed, and often surrendered to be scourged, maimed and tortured by the ruffian traitors, who pretend to own them. We complain that a large proportion of our regular Army Officers, with many of the Volunteers, evince far more solicitude to uphold slavery than to put down the Rebellion. And finally, we complain that you, Mr. President, elected as a Republican, knowing well what an abomination Slavery is, and how emphatically it is the core and essence of this atrocious Rebellion, seem never to interfere with those atrocities, and never give a direction to your military subordinates, which does not appear to have been conceived in the interest of slavery rather than of freedom. . . .

We complain that those who have . . . escaped to us, avowing a willingness to do for us whatever might be required, have been brutally and madly repulsed.

VIII. On the face of this wide earth, Mr. President, there is not one disinterested, determined, intelligent champion of the Union cause who does not feel that all attempts to put down the Rebellion and at the same time uphold its inciting cause are preposterous and futile—that the Rebellion, if crushed out to-morrow, would be renewed within a year if slavery were left in full vigor—that Army Officers who remain to this day devoted to slavery can at best be but half-way loyal to the Union—and that every hour of deference to slavery is an hour of added and deepened peril to the Union. I appeal to the testimony of your ambassadors in Europe. It is freely at your service, not at mine. Ask them to tell you candidly whether the seeming subserviency of your policy to the slaveholding, slavery-upholding interest, is not the perplexity, the despair of statesmen of all parties, and be admonished by the general answer.

IX. I close as I began with the statement that what an immense majority of the loyal millions of your countrymen require of you is a frank, declared, unqualified, ungrudging execution of the laws of the land, more especially of the Confiscation Act. That Act gives freedom to the slaves of Rebels coming within our lines, or whom those lines may at any time inclose—we ask you to render it due obedience by publicly requiring all your subordinates to recognize and obey it. The Rebels are everywhere using the late anti-negro riots in the North, as they have long used your officers' treatment of negroes in the South, to convince the slaves that they have nothing to hope from a Union success—that we mean in that case to sell them into a bitterer bondage to defray the cost of the war. Let them impress this as a truth on the great mass of their ignorant and credulous bondmen, and the Union will never be restored—never. We cannot conquer ten millions of people united in solid phalanx against us, powerfully aided by Northern sympathizers and European allies. We must have scouts, guides, spies, cooks, teamsters, diggers, and choppers, from the blacks of the South, whether we allow them to fight for us or not, or we shall be baffled and repelled. As one of the millions who would gladly have avoided this struggle at any sacrifice but that of principal [*sic*] and honor, but who now feel that the triumph of the Union is indispensable not only to the existence of our country, but to the well-being of mankind, I entreat you to render a hearty and unequivocal obedience to the law of the land.

Yours,
Horace Greeley.
New York, August 19, 1862

Lincoln's Reply to Mr. Greeley

Executive Mansion,
Washington, August 22, 1862

Hon. Horace Greeley:

Dear Sir

I have just read yours of the 19th. addressed to myself through the New-York Tribune. If there be in it any statements, or assumptions of fact, which I may know to be erroneous, I do not, now and here, controvert them. If there be in it any inferences which I may believe to be falsely drawn, I do not now and here, argue against them. If there be perceptable in it an impatient and dictatorial tone, I waive it in deference to an old friend, whose heart I have always supposed to be right.

As to the policy I "seem to be pursuing" as you say, I have not meant to leave any one in doubt.

I would save the Union. I would save it the shortest way under the Constitution. The sooner the national authority can be restored; the nearer the Union will be "the Union as it was." If there be those who would not save the Union, unless they could at the same time *save* slavery, I do not agree with them. If there be those who would not save the Union unless they could at the same time *destroy* slavery, I do not agree with them. My paramount object in this struggle *is* to save the Union, and is *not* either to save or destroy slavery. If I could save the Union without freeing *any* slave, I would do it, and if I could save it by freeing *all* the slaves, I would do it; and if I could save it by freeing some and leaving others alone I would also do that. What I do about slavery, and the colored race, I do because I believe it helps to save the Union; and what I forbear, I forbear because I do *not* believe it would help to save the Union. I shall do *less* whenever I shall believe what I am doing hurts the cause, and I shall do *more* whenever I shall believe doing more will help the cause. I shall try to correct errors when shown to be errors; and I shall adopt new views so far as they shall appear to be true views.

I have here stated my purpose according to my view of *official* duty; and I intend no modification of my oft-expressed *personal* wish that all men, every where could be free.

Yours,

A. Lincoln

Chapter 2

The Emancipation Proclamation's Effect on the Civil War

1

The Emancipation Proclamation Restored America's Reputation in the World

Charles Sumner

A staunch advocate of the immediate abolition of slavery, Republican senator from Massachusetts Charles Sumner praised Lincoln for the Preliminary Emancipation Proclamation. The following article is excerpted from his speech at Boston's Faneuil Hall on October 6, 1862, in which Sumner claims that the proclamation has infused a new sense of moral purpose into the war, negating claims made by Europeans that the war was being fought for imperial notions of "empire" engendered by the North and for "independence" by the South. Rather than signaling the demise of the Union as predicted by Europeans, Summer proclaims that the preliminary proclamation had ensured the republic will be one: "Liberty and Union, now and forever, one and inseparable."

Thank God that I live to enjoy this day! Thank God that my eyes have not closed without seeing this great salvation! The skies are brighter and the air is purer now that Slavery is handed over to judgment.

By the proclamation of the President, all persons held as slaves January 1, 1863, within any State or designated part of a State, the people whereof shall then be in rebellion against

Charles Sumner, speech at Faneuil Hall, October 6, 1862.

the United States, shall be then, thenceforward, and forever free; and the Executive Government of the United States, including the military and naval authority thereof, will recognize and maintain the freedom of such persons, and will do no act or acts to repress such persons, or any of them, in any efforts they may make for their actual freedom. Beyond these most effective words, which do not go into operation before the new year, are other words of immediate operation, constituting a present edict of Emancipation. The President recites the recent Acts of Congress applicable to this question, and calls upon all persons in the military and naval service to observe, obey, and enforce them. But these Acts provide that all slaves of Rebels, taking refuge within the lines of our army, all slaves captured from Rebels or deserted by them, and all slaves found within any place occupied by Rebel forces and afterwards occupied by forces of the United States, shall be forever free of servitude, and not again held as slaves; and these Acts further provide, that no person in the military or naval service shall, under any pretence whatever, assume to decide on the validity of any claim to a slave, or surrender any such person to his claimant, on pain of being dismissed from the service: so that by these Acts, now proclaimed by the President, Freedom is practically secured to all who find shelter within our lines, and the glorious flag of the Union, wherever it floats, becomes the flag of Freedom. . . .

Emancipation has begun, and our country is already elevated and glorified.

And now, thank God, the word is spoken!—greater word was seldom spoken. Emancipation has begun, and our country is already elevated and glorified. The war has not changed in *object*, but it has changed in *character.* Its object now, as at the beginning, is simply to put down the Rebellion; but its character is derived from the new force at length enlisted, stamping itself upon all that is done, and absorbing the whole war to itself. Vain will it be again to delude European nations into foolish belief that Slavery has nothing to do with the war, that it is a war for empire on one side and independence on the other, and that all generous ideas are on the side of the Rebellion. And vain, also, will be that other European cry,—whether from an intemperate press or the cautious lips of statesmen,—that separation is inevitable, and that our Government is doomed to witness the dismemberment of the Republic. With this new alliance; such forebodings will be falsified, the wishes of the fathers will be fulfilled, and the rights of human nature, which were the declared object of our Revolution, vindicated. Thus inspired, the sword of Washington—that sword which, according to his last will and testament, was to be drawn only in self-defence, or in defence of country and its rights—will once more marshal our armies to victory, while the national flag, wherever it floats, will give freedom to all beneath its folds, and the proud inscription be at last triumphantly verified: "Liberty and Union, now and forever, one and inseparable."

But, fellow-citizens, the war we wage is not merely for ourselves, it is for all mankind. Slavery yet lingers in Brazil, and beneath the Spanish flag in those two golden possessions, Cuba and Porto Rico; but nowhere can it survive extinction here. Therefore we conquer for Liberty everywhere. In ending Slavery here we open its gates all over the world, and let the oppressed go free. Nor is this all. In saving the Republic we save Civilization. Man throughout his long pilgrimage on earth has been compelled to suffer much, but Slavery is the heaviest burden he has been called to bear: it is the only burden our country has been called to bear. Let it drop, and this happy Republic, with humanity in its train, all changed in raiment and in countenance, like the Christian Pilgrim, will hurry upward to the celestial gate. If thus far our example has failed, it is simply because of Slavery. Vain to proclaim our unparalleled prosperity, the comfort diffused among a numerous people, resources without stint, or even the education of our children; the enemies of the Republic had but to say, "There is Slavery," and our example became powerless. But let Slavery disappear, and the same example will be of irresistible might. Without firing a gun or writing a despatch, it will revolutionize the world.

2

The Emancipation Proclamation Proves the Union Wants to Destroy the South

Jefferson Davis

President of the Confederacy Jefferson Davis had been a Democratic senator from Mississippi and U.S. secretary of war under President Franklin Pierce. In a speech to the joint session of the Senate and House of Representatives of the Confederate States of America in Richmond on January 21, 1863, from which the following is excerpted, Davis responds to Lincoln's final Emancipation Proclamation. He states that the proclamation is clear evidence that the Union's primary objective is to abolish slavery. As such, the proclamation will only serve to further isolate and separate the South from the Union.

The public journals of the North have been received, containing a proclamation, dated on the 1st day of the present month, signed by the President of the United States, in which he orders and declares all slaves within ten of the States of the Confederacy to be free, except such as are found within certain districts now occupied in part by the armed forces of the enemy. We may well leave it to the instincts of that common humanity which a beneficent Creator has implanted in the breasts of our fellowmen of all countries to pass judgement on a measure by which several

Jefferson Davis, address before the Senate and House of Representatives of the Confederate States of America, Richmond, Virginia, January 21, 1863.

millions of human beings of an inferior race, peaceful and contended [*sic*] laborers in their sphere, are doomed to extermination, while at the same time they are encouraged to a general assassination of their masters by the insidious recommendation "to abstain from violence unless in necessary self-defense." Our own detestation of those who have attempted the most execrable measure recorded in the history of guilty man is tempered by profound contempt for the impotent rage which it discloses. So far as regards the action of this Government on such criminals as may attempt its execution, I confine myself to informing you that I shall, unless in your wisdom you deem some other course more expedient, deliver to the several State authorities all commissioned officers of the United States that may hereafter be captured by our forces in any of the States embraced in the proclamation, that they may be dealt within in accordance with the laws of those States providing for the punishment of criminals engaged in exciting servile insurrection. The enlisted soldiers I shall continue to treat as unwilling instruments in the commission of these crimes, and shall direct their discharge and return to their homes on the proper and usual parole.

Our own detestation of those who have attempted the most execrable measure recorded in the history of guilty man is tempered by profound contempt.

In its political aspect this measure possesses great significance, and to it in this light I invite your attention. It affords to our whole people the complete and crowning proof of the true nature of the designs of the party which elevated to power the present occupant of the Presidential chair at Washington and which sought to conceal its purpose by every variety of artful device and by the perfidious use of the most solemn and repeated pledges on every possible occasion. . . .

Both before and after the actual commencement of hostilities the President of the United States repeated in formal official communication to the Cabinets of Great Britain and France that he was utterly without constitutional power to do the act which he has just committed, and that in no possible event, whether the secession of these States resulted in the establishment of a separate Confederacy or in the restoration of the Union, was there any authority by virtue of which he could either restore a disaffected State to the Union by force of arms or make any change in any of its institutions. I refer especially for verification of this assertion to the dispatches addressed by the Secretary of State of the United States, under direction of the President, to the Ministers of the United States at London and Paris, under date of 10th and 22d of April, 1861.

The people of this Confederacy, then, cannot fail to receive this proclamation as the fullest vindication of their own sagacity in forseeing the uses to which the dominant party in the United States intended from the beginning to apply their power, nor can they cease to remember with devout thankfulness that it is to their own vigilance in resisting the first stealthy progress of approaching despotism that they owe their escape from consequences now apparent to the most skeptical. This proclamation will have another salutary effect in calming the fears of those who have constantly evinced the apprehension that this war might end by some reconstruction of the Old Union or some renewal of close political relations with the United States. These fears have never been shared by me, nor have I ever been able to perceive on what basis they could rest. But the proclamation affords the fullest guarantee of the impossibility of such a result; it has established a state of things which can lead to but one of three possible consequences—the extermination of the slaves, the exile of the whole white population from the Confederacy, or absolute and total separation of these States from the United States.

This proclamation is also an authentic statement by the Government of the United States of its inability to subjugate the South by force of arms, and as such must be accepted by neutral nations, which can no longer find any justification in withholding our just claims to formal recognition. It is also in effect an intimation to the people of the North that they must prepare to submit to a separation, now become inevitable, for that people are too acute not to understand a restoration of the Union has been rendered forever impossible by the adoption of a measure which from its very nature neither admits a retraction nor can coexist with union.

3

The Emancipation Proclamation Will Hasten the End of the War

Abraham Lincoln

After issuing the Emancipation Proclamation, President Lincoln was invited to speak at a Union rally in his hometown of Springfield, Illinois. Unable to attend, Lincoln wrote a letter to a close friend, James C. Conkling, dated August 26, 1863, from which the following is excerpted, to be read at the proposed rally. In an effort to dispel Union members' disenchantment with the Emancipation Proclamation, Lincoln addressed several issues that were of concern to them. Lincoln states that the most important principle of his proclamation is that all men should be free. Second, Lincoln writes that the proclamation would deliver the "heaviest blow yet" to rebel forces. It became clear to Lincoln and his generals that the Emancipation Proclamation signaled the demise of slavery in the United States, a decision ratified by the passage of the Thirteenth Amendment in December 1865.

Abraham Lincoln, letter to James C. Conkling, August 26, 1863.

Executive Mansion,
Washington, August 26, 1863.

Hon. James C. Conkling
My Dear Sir.

Your letter inviting me to attend a mass-meeting of unconditional Unionmen, to be held at the Capitol of Illinois, on the 3d day of September, has been received.

It would be very agreeable to me, to thus meet my old friends, at my own home; but I can not, just now, be absent from here, so long as a visit there, would require.

The meeting is to be of all those who maintain unconditional devotion to the Union; and I am sure my old political friends will thank me for tendering, as I do, the nation's gratitude to those other noble men, whom no partizan malice, or partizan hope, can make false to the nation's life. . . .

I certainly wish that all men could be free, while I suppose you do not.

But to be plain, you are dissatisfied with me about the negro. Quite likely there is a difference of opinion between you and myself upon that subject. I certainly wish that all men could be free, while I suppose you do not. Yet I have neither adopted, nor proposed any measure, which is not consistent with even your view, provided you are for the Union. I suggested compensated emancipation; to which you replied you wished not to be taxed to buy negroes. But I had not asked you to be taxed to buy negroes, except in such way, as to save you from greater taxation to save the Union exclusively by other means.

The Proclamation Is Not Unconstitutional

You dislike the emancipation proclamation; and, perhaps, would have it retracted. You say it is unconstitutional—I think differently. I think the constitution invests its Commander-in-chief, with the law of war, in time of war. The most that can be said, if so much, is, that slaves are property. Is there—has there ever been—any question that by the law of war, property, both of enemies and friends, may be taken when needed? And is it not needed whenever taking it, helps us, or hurts the enemy? Armies, the world over, destroy enemies' property when they can not use it; and even destroy their own to keep it from the enemy. Civilized belligerents do all in their power to help themselves, or hurt the enemy, except a few things regarded as barbarous or cruel. Among the exceptions are the massacre of vanquished foes, and non-combatants, male and female.

The emancipation policy and the use of the colored troops constitute the heaviest blow yet dealt to the Rebellion.

But the proclamation, as law, either is valid, or is not valid. If it is not valid, it needs no retraction. If it is valid, it can not be retracted, any more than the dead can be brought to life. Some of you profess to think its retraction would operate favorably for the Union. Why better *after* the retraction, than *before* the issue? There was more than a year and a half of trial to suppress the rebellion before the proclamation issued, the last one hundred days of which passed under an explicit notice that it was coming, unless averted by those in revolt, returning to their allegiance. The war has certainly progressed as favorably for us, since the issue of proclamation as before. I know, as fully as one can know the opinions of others, that some of the commanders of our armies in the field who have given us our most important successes believe the emancipation policy and the use of the colored troops constitute the heaviest blow yet dealt to the Rebellion, and that at least one of these important successes could not have been achieved when it was but for the aid of black soldiers. Among the commanders holding these views are some who have never had any affinity with what is called abolitionism or with the Republican party policies but who held them purely as military opinions. I submit these opinions as being entitled to some weight against the objections often urged that emancipation and arming the blacks are unwise as military measures and were not adopted as such in good faith.

The Proclamation Helps Save the Union

You say you will not fight to free negroes. Some of them seem willing to fight for you; but, no matter. Fight you, then, exclusively to save the Union. I issued the proclamation on purpose to aid you in saving the Union. Whenever you shall have conquered all resistence to the Union, if I shall urge you to continue fighting, it will be an apt time, then, for you to declare you will not fight to free negroes.

Peace does not appear so distant as it did. I hope it will come soon, and come to stay.

I thought that in your struggle for the Union, to whatever extent the negroes should cease helping the enemy, to that extent it weakened the enemy in his resistence to you. Do you think differently? I thought that whatever negroes can be got to do as soldiers, leaves just so much less for white soldiers to do, in saving the Union. Does it appear otherwise to you? But negroes, like other people, act upon motives. Why should they do any thing for us, if we will do nothing for them? If they stake their lives for us, they must be prompted by the strongest motive—even the promise of freedom. And the promise being made, must be kept.

The signs look better. The Father of Waters again goes unvexed to the sea. Thanks to the great Northwest for it. Nor yet wholly to them. Three hundred miles up, they met New England, Empire, Key-stone, and Jersey, hewing their way right and left. The Sunny South too, in more colors than one, also lent a hand. On the spot, their part of the history was jotted down in black and white. The job was a great national one; and let none be banned who bore an honorable part in it. And while those who have cleared the great river may well be proud, even that is not all. It is hard to say that anything has been more bravely, and well done, than at Antietam, Murfreesboro, Gettysburg, and on many fields of lesser note. Nor must Uncle Sam's web-feet be forgotten. At all the watery margins they have been present. Not only on the deep sea, the broad bay, and the rapid river, but also up the narrow muddy bayou, and wherever the ground was a little damp, they have been, and made their tracks. Thanks to all. For the great republic—for the principle it lives by, and keeps alive—for man's vast future—thanks to all.

Peace does not appear so distant as it did. I hope it will come soon, and come to stay; and so come as to be worth the keeping in all future time. It will then have been proved that, among free men, there can be no successful appeal from the ballot to the bullet; and that they who take such appeal are sure to lose their case, and pay the cost. And then, there will be some black men who can remember that, with silent tongue, and clenched teeth, and steady eye, and well-poised bayonnet, they have helped mankind on to this great consummation; while, I fear, there will be some white ones, unable to forget that, with malignant heart, and deceitful speech, they strove to hinder it.

Still, let us not be over-sanguine of a speedy final triumph. Let us be quite sober. Let us diligently apply the means, never doubting that a just God, in his own good time, will give us the rightful result.

Yours very truly

A. Lincoln

4

The Emancipation Proclamation Is Unenforceable

Valley Spirit

Newspapers published during the Civil War provide interesting perspectives on the debate surrounding the Emancipation Proclamation. Unlike the newspapers of today, Civil War–era newspapers usually favored a clear side, either Democratic or Republican. The language was often verbose and hostile. In the October 1, 1862, issue of the *Valley Spirit*, excerpted here, the editors express dismay at Lincoln's decision to issue the Emancipation Proclamation. They assert that since Lincoln could not enforce the Constitution in rebel states, the Emancipation Proclamation, for all intents and purposes, is also unenforceable.

The editors express their deep disappointment with Lincoln's Emancipation Proclamation. They had hoped that he would ignore the advice of radicals, and they had praised every evidence of his conservative tendencies. Now, however, the editors see that Lincoln has thrown his lot in with the radicals. The Proclamation will have little practical effect, they note, except to alienate Unionist Southerners as well as slaveholders in the border states. . . .

The great agony of the radicals is over. They clamored for a proclamation until they succeeded. They besieged the President on all sides, and waged an incessant war upon him

Valley Spirit, "The President's Proclamation," October 1, 1862.

for months, until at last he succumbed to the "pressure" and issued a proclamation proclaiming unconditional freedom to all the slaves in the seceded States after the first day of January next. Where the President pretends to find his authority for issuing such a proclamation, he does not deign to inform us. This new policy is to be the great panacea for all our ills, and is to kill the rebellion at one blow. We shall soon see the fruits of the policy and know from practical experience, what abolition philosophy is worth. In the meantime we must be permitted to hold the same views we have ever held on this subject, until we are convinced to the contrary by practical results.

The conservative men of the country have been greatly disappointed in this action of the President.

The conservative men of the country have been greatly disappointed in this action of the President. They had been persuaded that he was a man of honest intentions and desired to do what was best for his country. They hoped, even sometimes against hope, that he would eventually see the true ground of his position, discard the mad counsels and revolutionary teachings of the radical men of his party, plant himself firmly upon the pillars of the Constitution, and make an earnest effort to save the country. They caught at every exhibition of conservatism in the President to strengthen this opinion, and were prompt in commending and endorsing every act of his tending to strengthen and promote the great cause in which the country is engaged, where the abolitionists who are now in ecstacies [*sic*] over his recent proclamation, either treated him with silent contempt or broke out in open murmurs of discontent and opposition. Yet in the face of these facts the President has given way to their clamor, and thrown himself, body and soul, into the hands of the radical abolition faction, who have been seeking the ruin of the country for many years, and who have pronounced the Constitution a "league with death and a covenant with hell," and the honest and conservative masses of the free States and the loyal Union men of the Slave States, have been shamefully deceived, and the nation been made to bleed afresh at every pore through the weakness and imbecility of its chief executive officer.

A word as to the effect of this Proclamation. Practically it is not worth the paper it is written on. If the administration is unable to enforce the legitimate and Constitutional laws of the country, in the seceded States, how is this unconstitutional and foolish paper proclamation to be enforced? The President himself told the Chicago Delegation[1] that it would be inoperative, and could not free a single slave. The proposition is too absurd for a moment's serious consideration.

But there is another aspect in which this subject is all important, that of its bearing upon the loyal Union men of the slave States. They have suffered long and much for the sacred cause of the Union in their respective States. They persistently denied the allegations of the Secessionists that this was war on the part of the Government for the abolition of Slavery. This was the great argument of the Secessionists by which they were enabled to carry the people with them. The Union men planted themselves upon the broad principles of the Constitution, and bravely contended for the old Union and the old flag, with danger and death oftentimes staring them in the face, trusting in the good faith of the administration to sustain them. How have they been sustained. Alas! how President Lincoln, with one stroke of the pen, violates the plighted faith of the Government, and says to the whole southern people, that the Union men were wrong and the Secessionists were right. In no other way could Abraham Lincoln have done so much to strengthen and consolidate the rebellion. We have no doubt that Jefferson Davis would have given the last dollar in the Confederate Treasury to have just such a proclamation emanate from the President of the United States.

---

1. Lincoln gave a speech to a Chicago delegation of religious leaders in September 1862, arguing against making slavery an issue of the war.

Chapter **3**

Historical Assessment of the Emancipation Proclamation

1

The Effects of the Emancipation Proclamation and Lincoln's Legacy Are Mixed

Frederick Douglass

Influenced by nineteenth-century Protestant Christianity and ideas of the Enlightenment and Romanticism, Frederick Douglass was an abolitionist, a newspaper editor, a social reformer, and a fighter for civil rights. Although Douglass was a friend of Lincoln, his sentiments toward the Emancipation Proclamation were ambivalent. In the following excerpt from his speech at the dedication of the Freedmen's Monument on April 14, 1876, Douglass analyzes the proclamation. Douglass argues that although the Emancipation Proclamation was both revolutionary and visionary, Lincoln was concerned less with the sufferings of the African American slave than he was with the well-being of the white man.

Fellow-citizens, in what we have said and done today, and in what we may say and do hereafter, we disclaim everything like arrogance and assumption. We claim for ourselves no superior devotion to the character, history, and memory of the illustrious name whose monument we have here dedicated today. We fully comprehend the relation of

Frederick Douglass, speech at the dedication of the Freedmen's Monument, Washington, DC, April 14, 1876.

Abraham Lincoln both to ourselves and to the white people of the United States. Truth is proper and beautiful at all times and in all places, and it is never more proper and beautiful in any case than when speaking of a great public man whose example is likely to be commended for honor and imitation long after his departure to the solemn shades, the silent continents of eternity. It must be admitted, truth compels me to admit even here in the presence of the monument we have erected to his memory, Abraham Lincoln was not, in the fullest sense of the word, either our man or our model. In his interests, in his associations, in his habit of thought, and in his prejudices, he was a white man.

The White Man's President

He was preëminently the white man's President, entirely devoted to the welfare of white men. He was ready and willing at any time during the first years of his administration to deny, postpone, and sacrifice the rights of humanity in the colored people to promote the welfare of the white people of this country. In all his education and feeling he was an American of the Americans. He came into the Presidential chair upon one principle alone, namely, opposition to the extension of slavery. His arguments in furtherance of this policy had their motive and mainspring in his patriotic devotion to the interests of his own race. To protect, defend, and perpetuate slavery in the states where it existed Abraham Lincoln was not less ready than any other President to draw the sword of the nation. He was ready to execute all the supposed guarantees of the United States Constitution in favor of the slave system anywhere inside the slave states. He was willing to pursue, recapture, and send back the fugitive slave to his master, and to suppress a slave rising for liberty though his guilty master were already in arms against the Government. The race to which we belong were not the special objects of his consideration. Knowing this, I concede to you, my white fellow-citizens, a preëminence in this worship at once full and supreme. First, midst, and last, you and yours were the objects of his deepest affection and his most earnest solicitude. You are the children of Abraham Lincoln. We are at best only his step-children; children by adoption, children by forces of circumstances and necessity. To you it especially belongs to sound his praises, to preserve and perpetuate his memory, to multiply his statues, to hang his pictures high upon your walls, and commend his example, for to you he was a great and glorious friend and benefactor. Instead of supplanting you at his altar, we would exhort you to build high his monuments; let them be of the most costly material, of the most cunning workmanship; let their forms be symmetrical, beautiful, and perfect; let their bases be upon solid rocks, and their summits lean against the unchanging blue, overhanging sky, and let them endure forever! But while in the abundance of your wealth, and in the fullness of your just and patriotic devotion, you do all this, we entreat you to despise not the humble offering we this day unveil to view; for while Abraham Lincoln saved for you a country, he delivered us from a bondage, according to Jefferson, one hour of which was worse than ages of the oppression your fathers rose in rebellion to oppose. . . .

The race to which we belong were not the special objects of [Abraham Lincoln's] consideration.

I have said that President Lincoln was a white man, and shared the prejudices common to his countrymen towards the colored race. Looking back to his times and to the condition of his country, we are compelled to admit that this unfriendly feeling on his part may be safely set down as one element of his wonderful success in organizing the loyal American people for the tremendous conflict before them, and bringing them safely through that conflict. His great mission was to accomplish two things: first, to save his country from dismemberment and ruin; and, second, to free his country from the great crime of slavery. To do one or the other, or both, he must have the earnest sympathy and the powerful coöperation of his loyal fellow-countrymen. Without this primary and essential condition to success his efforts must have been vain and utterly fruitless. Had he put the abolition of slavery before the salvation of the Union, he would have inevitably driven from him a powerful class of the American people and rendered resistance to rebellion impossible. Viewed from the genuine abolition ground, Mr. Lincoln seemed tardy, cold, dull, and indifferent; but measuring him by the sentiment of his country, a sentiment he was bound as a statesman to consult, he was swift, zealous, radical, and determined.

Though Mr. Lincoln shared the prejudices of his white fellow-countrymen against the Negro, it is hardly necessary to say that in his heart of hearts he loathed and hated slavery. . . . The man who could say, "Fondly do we hope, fervently do we pray, that this mighty scourge of war shall soon pass away, yet if God wills it continue till all the wealth piled by two hundred years of bondage shall have been wasted, and each drop of blood drawn by the lash shall have been paid for by one drawn by the sword, the judgments of the Lord are true and righteous altogether," gives all needed proof of his feeling on the subject of slavery. He was willing, while the South was loyal, that it should have its pound of flesh, because he thought that it was so nominated in the bond; but farther than this no earthly power could make him go. . . .

Abraham Lincoln was clear in his duty and had an oath in heaven.

Happily for the country, happily for you and for me, the judgment of James Buchanan, the patrician, was not the judgment of Abraham Lincoln, the plebeian. He brought his strong common sense, sharpened in the school of adversity, to bear upon the question. He did not hesitate, he did not doubt, he did not falter; but at once resolved that at whatever peril, at whatever cost, the union of the States should be preserved. A patriot himself, his faith was strong and unwavering in the patriotism of his countrymen. Timid men said before Mr. Lincoln's inauguration that we had seen the last President of the United States. A voice in influential quarters said, "Let the Union slide." Some said that a Union maintained by the sword was worthless. Others said a rebellion of 8,000,000 cannot be suppressed; but in the midst of all this tumult and timidity, and against all this, Abraham Lincoln was clear in his duty and had an oath in heaven. He calmly and bravely heard the voice of doubt and fear all around him; but he had an oath in heaven, and there was not power enough on earth to make this honest boatman, backwoodsman, and broad-handed splitter of rails evade or violate the sacred oath. He had not been schooled in the ethics of slavery; his plain life had favored his love of truth. He had not been taught that treason and perjury were the proof of honor and honesty. His moral training was against his saying one thing when he meant another. The trust that Abraham Lincoln had in himself and in the people was surprising and grand, but it was also enlightened and well founded. He knew the American people better than they knew themselves, and his truth was based upon this knowledge. . . .

Had Abraham Lincoln died from any of the numerous ills to which flesh is heir; had he reached that good old age of which his vigorous constitution and his temperate habits gave promise; had he been permitted to see the end of his great work; had the solemn curtain of death come down but gradually—we should still have been smitten with heavy grief, and treasured his name lovingly. But dying as he did die, by the red hand of violence, killed, assassinated, taken off without warning, not because of personal hate—for no man who knew Abraham Lincoln could hate him—but because of his fidelity to union and liberty, he is doubly dear to us, and his memory will be precious forever.

2

The Emancipation Proclamation Did Not End Slavery

Richard Hofstadter

Richard Hofstadter is an American political historian. He spent most of his career as a professor at Columbia University. Hofstadter won a Pulitzer Prize for history for his book *The Age of Reform: From Bryan to FDR* (1955). In his most popular book, *American Political Tradition and the Men Who Made It*, from which the following viewpoint is excerpted, Hofstadter argues that Lincoln's attempts to free the slaves were disingenuous at best. He asserts that Lincoln's proposed compensated emancipation plan, designed to reimburse border states that would voluntarily emancipate slaves, was less concerned with the moral imperative of destroying slavery than it was with the actual monetary savings that would accrue from not taking military action against border states. Furthermore, Hofstadter claims that Lincoln's primary concern was the fate of the "free white worker" and the threat posed by freed slaves to the development of capitalism. According to Hofstadter, it was precisely Lincoln's notion of repatriation and deportation of African Americans that would, in Lincoln's estimation, augment the requirement for, and earnings of, white workers. Hofstadter claims, moreover, that Lincoln decided to issue the Emancipation Proclamation only after all his other policies had failed. Even at that, he argues, the proclamation accomplished nothing "beyond its propaganda value" because it failed to condemn the evils of human bondage and the immense suffering endured by African American slaves.

L incoln had genuine constitutional scruples, but his conservatism in everything pertaining to slavery was also dictated by political and strategic considerations.

To say that Lincoln's approach to the slavery question was governed by his penchant for philosophic resignation is not to say that he had no policy of his own. His program flowed from his conception that his role was to be a moderator of extremes in public sentiment. It called for compensated emancipation (at first in the loyal border states) assisted by federal funds, to be followed at length by deportation and colonization of the freed Negroes. To a member of the Senate he wrote in 1862 that the cost of freeing with compensation all slaves in the four border states and the District of Columbia, at an average price of four hundred dollars per slave, would come to less than the cost of eighty-seven days of the war. Further, he believed that taking such action would shorten the war by more than eighty-seven days and "thus be an actual saving of expense." Despite the gross note of calculation at the end (one rescues 432,000 human beings from slavery and it turns out to be a saving of expense), the proposal was a reasonable and statesmanlike one, and it is incredible that the intransigence of all but one of the states involved should have consigned it to defeat.

The alternative idea of colonizing the Negroes abroad was and always had been pathetic. There had been in existence for a generation an active movement to colonize the slaves, but it had not sent out of the country more than the tiniest fraction of the annual increase of the slave population. By 1860 its fantastic character must have been evident to every American who was not determined to deceive himself. Nevertheless, when a deputation of colored men came to see Lincoln in the summer of 1862, he tried to persuade them to set up a colony in Central America, which, he said, stood on one of the world's highways and provided a country of "great natural resources and advantages." "If I could find twenty-five able-bodied men, with a mixture of women and children," he added, with marvelous naïveté, ". . . I could make a successful commencement."

Plainly Lincoln was, as always, thinking primarily of the free white worker: the Negro was secondary. The submerged whites of the South and the wage workers of the North feared the prospect of competing with the labor of liberated blacks. The venerable idea of deporting emancipated Negroes, fantastic though it was, grew logically out of a caste psychology in a competitive labor market. Lincoln assured Congress that emancipation would not lower wage standards of white labor even if the freedmen were not deported. But if they were deported, "enhanced wages to white labor is mathematically certain. . . . Reduce the supply of black labor by colonizing the black laborer out of the country, and by precisely so much you increase the demand for, and wages of, white labor."

Lincoln was, as always, thinking primarily of the free white worker.

In the summer of 1862 Congress passed a Confiscation Act providing that the slaves of all persons supporting the rebellion should be forever free. The Radicals had also proposed to make the measure retroactive and to provide for permanent forfeiture of the real estate of rebels. Lincoln was adamant about these features, and had no enthusiasm for the act in general, but finally signed a bill that had been modified according to his demands. Even with these concessions the Radicals had scored a triumph and forced Lincoln part way toward emancipation. He had prevented them from destroying the landed basis of the Southern aristocracy, but he had put his signature, however reluctantly, to a measure that freed the slaves of all persons found guilty of disloyalty; freed them on paper, at least, for the act was unenforceable during the war. It also guaranteed that escaped slaves would no longer be sent back to work for disloyal masters, and in this respect freed some slaves in reality.

When Lincoln at last determined, in July 1862, to move toward emancipation, it was only after all his other policies had failed. The Crittenden Resolution had been rejected, the border states had quashed his plan of compensated emancipation, his generals were still floundering, and he had already lost the support of great numbers of conservatives. The Proclamation became necessary to hold his remaining supporters and to forestall—so he believed—English recognition of the Confederacy. "I would save the Union," he wrote in answer to Horace Greeley's cry for emancipation. ". . . If I could save the Union without freeing any slave, I would do it; and if I could do it by freeing all the slaves, I would do it." In the end, freeing all the slaves seemed necessary.

It was evidently an unhappy frame of mind in which Lincoln resorted to the Emancipation Proclamation. "Things had gone from bad to worse," he told the artist F.B. Carpenter a year later, "until I felt that we had reached the end of our rope on the plan of operations we had been pursuing; that we had about played our last card, and must change our tactics, or lose the game. I now determined upon the adoption of the emancipation policy. . . ." The passage has a wretched tone: things had gone from bad to worse, and as a result the slaves were to be declared free!

The Emancipation Proclamation . . . had all the moral grandeur of a bill of lading.

The Emancipation Proclamation of January 1, 1863 had all the moral grandeur of a bill of lading. It contained no indictment of slavery, but simply based emancipation on "military necessity." It expressly omitted the loyal slave states from its terms. Finally, it did not in fact free any slaves. For it excluded by detailed enumeration from the sphere covered in the Proclamation all the counties in Virginia and parishes in Louisiana that were occupied by Union troops and into which the government actually had the power to bring freedom. It simply declared free all slaves in "the States and parts of States" where the people were in rebellion—that is to say, precisely where its effect could not reach. Beyond its propaganda value the Proclamation added nothing to what Congress had already done in the Confiscation Act.

[Secretary of State William Henry] Seward remarked of the Proclamation: "We show our sympathy with slavery by emancipating the slaves when we cannot reach them and holding them in bondage where we can set them free." The London *Spectator* gibed: "The principle is not that a human being cannot justly own another, but that he cannot own him unless he is loyal to the United States."

But the Proclamation was what it was because the average sentiments of the American Unionist of 1862 were what they were. Had the political strategy of the moment called for a momentous human document of the stature of the Declaration of Independence, Lincoln could have risen to the occasion. Perhaps the largest reasonable indictment of him is simply that in such matters he was a follower and not a leader of public opinion. It may be that there was in Lincoln something of the old Kentucky poor white, whose regard for the slaves was more akin to his feeling for tortured animals than it was to his feeling, say, for the common white man of the North. But it is only the intensity and not the genuiness of his antislavery sentiments that can be doubted. His conservatism arose in part from a sound sense for the pace of historical change. He knew that formal freedom for the Negro, coming suddenly and without preparation, would not be real freedom, and in this respect he understood the slavery question better than most of the Radicals, just as they had understood better than he the revolutionary dynamics of the war.

For all its limitations, the Emancipation Proclamation probably made genuine emancipation inevitable. In all but five of the states freedom was accomplished in fact through the thirteenth amendment. Lincoln's own part in the passing of this amendment was critical. He used all his influence to get the measure the necessary two-thirds vote in the House of Representatives, and it was finally carried by a margin of three votes. Without his influence the amendment might have been long delayed, though it is hardly conceivable that it could have been held off indefinitely. Such claim as he may have to be remembered as an Emancipator perhaps rests more justly on his behind-the-scenes activity for the thirteenth amendment than on the Proclamation itself. It was the Proclamation, however, that had psychological value, and before the amendment was passed, Lincoln had already become the personal symbol of freedom. Believing that he was called only to conserve, he had turned liberator in spite of himself:

"I claim not to have controlled events but confess plainly that events have controlled me."

3

The Emancipation Proclamation Ended Slavery

Allen C. Guelzo

Allen C. Guelzo is the Grace F. Kea Professor of American History at Eastern College and cowinner of the Lincoln Prize for his 1999 biography *Abraham Lincoln: Redeemer President.* In *Lincoln's Emancipation Proclamation: The End of Slavery,* from which this essay is excerpted, Guelzo argues, "Without the legal freedom conferred first by the Emancipation Proclamation, no runaway slave would have remained self-emancipated for very long." He claims that even during the first years of the war, slave owners would march through enemy lines with the arm of the law at their side seeking to reclaim their runaway slaves. The Emancipation Proclamation changed all that. In declaring emancipation a military necessity, Guelzo states, Union soldiers could now legally liberate slaves across the heartland of the Confederacy. In addition, runaway slaves could legally lay claim to their freedom and thus could not be arrested or detained as contraband.

Was emancipation really a military asset? The answer had to be *yes,* if Lincoln's argument for including emancipation among the military necessities was to have any staying power. In the summer of 1863, the jury on that question was still out. For more than a year and a half, a slow leakage of contrabands and fugitives had been trickling northwards into the Union Army's lines, then into refugee camps, and, for a favored few, into freedom in the North. They were drawn mostly from the upper South and the Border, and the agitation they raised among both Northerners and Southerners was greatly out of proportion to their actual numbers. All told, there may have been as few as 60,000 contrabands and other runaways in Union hands by September of 1862, and probably not more than 200,000—in other words, not more than 5 percent of the total number of enslaved blacks in the Confederacy and the Border. Many slaves seized the opportunity of the war's confusion to grab at whatever freedom the circumstances offered, but the halfheartedness of Union generals, the ineffectiveness of the Confiscation Acts, and the simple risks involved kept the numbers of those fugitives few. "Every time a bunch of No'thern sojers would come through they would tell us we was free and we'd begin celebratin'," remembered Ambrose Douglass, a slave in North Carolina. But "before we would get through somebody else would tell us to go back to work, and we would go. Some of us wanted to jine up with the army, but we didn't know who was goin' to win and didn't take no chances."

Escape Was Not Emancipation

Soon enough, the fugitives learned that running away might get a slave out of the master's control, but that this was not the same thing as emancipation. Escape from bondage was temporary and could disappear the moment a master showed up with paperwork in his hand, demonstrating loyalty to the federal government and ownership of a slave. Even where white soldiers displayed the best of intentions, blacks knew that they were only passing through and could not always be counted on to come to the aid of slave rebels. "I spose dat you'se true," commented one Georgia slave dryly as Sherman marched to the sea, "but, massa, you'se 'll go way to-morrow, and anudder white man'll come."

The Emancipation Proclamation radically altered this situation. Union soldiers now had the power to declare emancipation, and not just to encourage flight, to slaves across the Confederacy. A column of soldiers passed John McCline's home north of Nashville in December 1862 and urged him to "come on, Johnny, and go with us . . . and we will set you free." Victoria Perry watched "a Yankee come by the house" and call the slaves together so that a Union officer could announce "all we were free. My mother shouted, 'The Lord be praised.'" It scarcely mattered how word of the Proclamation arrived, whether informally along the slave grapevine or more openly, as in the case of James Simms of Savannah, who brought copies of the Proclamation from Virginia to distribute among Savannah's blacks. The superintendent of contrabands at Fortress Monroe was surprised to find "some men who came here from North Carolina" already "knew all about the Proclamation." A rebel prisoner at Fortress Monroe told him "that one of his negroes had told him of the proclamation five days before he heard it in any other way," while others claimed that "their negroes gave them their first information" of the proclamation. One Union soldier believed that "intelligence of 'Massa' Linkum's emancipation proclamation had doubtless reached every Negro household from Mason and Dixon's line to the Gulf of Mexico."

The damage wrought by the Proclamation went . . . like a stake in the heart of slavery's collective psyche.

In many instances, slaveowners tried to suppress news of the Proclamation, and some were successful enough that their slaves learned nothing about emancipation until the arrival of Union soldiers or even after the conclusion of the war. . . . Even in the areas that were technically exempt, the Proclamation made "the condition of things . . . unsettled, revolutionary, with nothing clearly defined, neither slave nor slaveholder having any rights which they felt bound mutually to respect." Once the Proclamation was issued, the former slave H.C. Bruce noticed that "slave property in the state of Missouri was almost a dead weight to the owner; he could not sell because there were no buyers." Although Missouri was exempt from emancipation, the Proclamation still managed to destabilize slavery even where it remained legal. "All the negroes in this country will run off," predicted a Missouri secessionist at the end of October 1862, "they go in droves every night.". . .

The Proclamation would have accomplished enough in wartime terms just by conveying to the slaves a new legal

status that banished all obligation to their rebel masters. But
the damage wrought by the Proclamation went deeper, like
a stake in the heart of slavery's collective psyche, and the
dread grew in white Southerners as they beheld around
them people who would not consent any longer to be *things*.
Black war correspondent Thomas Morris Chester described
the Proclamation as a renovation of black humanity. It "pro-
tects the sanctity of the marriage relationship . . . justifies
the natural right of the mother over the disposition of her
daughters, and gives to the father the only claim which
Almighty God intended should be exercised by man over
his son" and "ends the days of oppression, cruelty and out-
rage, founded on complexion, and introduces an era of
emancipation, humanity and virtue, founded upon the principles of unerring justice."

Whether the Proclamation acted upon someone at once
or not until 1865, the word of its coming upset not only the
law of slavery but the personal humiliations it fastened on its
victims. For male slaves, emancipation meant an emergence
into a manhood that slavery had denied them. Freedom was
yearned for by some simply "because the treatment was so
bad," wrote Louis Hughes, but those who "had looked into
the matter" and understood the personal dynamic of slavery
looked for a more substantial transformation. . . .

---

*Emancipation was now securely wedged into the
war's equation as a sine qua non of victory.*

To experience emancipation was also to experience a
liberation from place, whether a plantation or a factory, and
that liberation also removed some key underpinnings of
Southern resistance. Emancipated slaves flocked to cities,
whether Northern cities, beyond the Union lines, or Southern cities once the war was over. . . .

That so few of the dire things promised for the Proclamation ever came true is a measure of Lincoln's skill as a legal draftsman and his determination to make the Proclamation proof against the political hounds that surrounded it.
That feat, real as it is, has tended to overshadow the things
that the Proclamation really did accomplish. Lincoln's critics
were quick to take William Seward's sarcasm one step further and claim that the Proclamation had never freed anyone

at all. "Where he has no power Mr. Lincoln will set the negroes free; where he retains power he will consider them as
slaves," said the London *Times*. The Proclamation was mere
political gesture, with no real force, "like a Chinaman beat-
ing his two swords together to frighten his enemy." But
sound and fury were not Lincoln's style, and whatever his
personal uncertainties about the legal standing of the Proclamation after the war, no one below the Mason-Dixon Line
had any doubts about its efficacy. In time, it would become
clear even to the nay-sayers that the Proclamation closed and
locked the door on any possibility that slavery could be tip-
toed around, or that the war could be fought as though slavery had nothing to do with it. In practical terms alone, Lincoln explained in 1864, trying to adopt "a different policy in
regard to the colored man, deprives us of his help, and this is
more than we can bear. . . . Throw it away, and the Union
goes with it." But it was also a matter of principle with Lincoln. It was bad faith of the worst imaginable sort to "retain
the service of these people with the express or implied un-
derstanding that upon the first convenient occasion, they are
to be re-enslaved. It *can* not be," and what was more important, "it *ought* not to be." But if, by some incredible circum-
stance, Congress did agree to negotiate an end to the war by
backtracking on the Proclamation, they would have to do so
without him as President. To abandon the Proclamation, he
told Congress in his annual message in December 1863,
"would be not only to relinquish a lever of power, but would
also be a cruel and an astounding breach of faith. I may add
at this point, that while I remain in my present position I
shall not attempt to retract or modify the emancipation
proclamation; nor shall I return to slavery any person who is
free by the terms of that proclamation, or by any of the acts
of Congress." He repeated that promise a year later, adding
for sharper effect, "If the people should, by whatever mode
or means, make it an Executive duty to re-enslave such persons, another, and not I, must be their instrument to perform
it." Emancipation was now securely wedged into the war's
equation as a sine qua non of victory.

"The Extinction of Slavery"

This was not just bluff. Slave runaways from the Confederacy now had a legal claim on freedom and could not be arrested as fugitives or interned as contrabands; every rebel

county, every rebel city, and every rebel state the Union armies overran became free territory for at least the duration of the war; prosecutions for violations of the Proclamation went forward in at least two documented cases while the war was in progress. "I hold that this Proclamation did, in law, free every slave in all the region it covered," declared Charles Drake, the antislavery Missouri Radical, and "on the very day it was issued." No one should "for a moment imagine that the Emancipation Proclamation had no force in law," warned the abolitionist Robert Dale Owen. "By that instrument three millions of slaves were legally set free." Their owners across the Confederacy might prevent them from exercising that freedom at that moment. But since when had laws lacked force simply for being prospective? Or for being obstructed by rebels? "It is true," Owen admitted, "that many of these people are working as slaves still; but in the eye of the law, they are freedmen. Our own right to freedom is not better than theirs." Even Montgomery Blair agreed, however reluctantly, that "the proclamation of the President . . . has announced the extinction of slavery."

4

Lincoln Had No Intention of Freeing the Slaves

Lerone Bennett Jr.

Lerone Bennett Jr. is a prolific African American writer and social historian who has authored several books, including: *Before the Mayflower: A History of Black America; What Manner of Man: A Biography of Martin Luther King; Pioneers in Protest: Black Power USA; The Human Side of Reconstruction, 1867–1877*; and *Great Moments in Black History*. Bennett was also on the editorial staff of *Ebony* magazine for more than fifty years. In his recent work *Forced into Glory: Abraham Lincoln's White Dream*, from which the following essay is excerpted, Bennett argues that the Emancipation Proclamation was a fraud. He states that in freeing slaves in rebel territory while holding them in bondage in Union-held territory, the Emancipation Proclamation was designed to curtail the immediate liberation of *all* slaves. According to Bennett, evidence suggests that Lincoln's real motive for the proclamation was not to free the slaves, but rather to keep them in bondage until he could rally support for his racist agenda: gradual emancipation and the deportation of blacks to countries outside the United States.

The testimony of sixteen thousand books and monographs to the contrary notwithstanding, Lincoln did *not* emancipate the slaves, greatly or otherwise. As for the Emancipation Proclamation, it was not a real emancipation proclamation at all, and did not liberate African-American slaves. John F. Hume, the Missouri antislavery leader who heard Lincoln speak in Alton [Illinois] and who looked him in the eye in the White House, said the Proclamation "did not . . . whatever it may have otherwise accomplished at the time it was issued, liberate a single slave."

Sources favorable to Lincoln were even more emphatic. Lincoln crony Henry Clay Whitney said the Proclamation was a mirage and that Lincoln knew it was a mirage. Secretary of State William Henry Seward, the No. 2 man in the administration, said the Proclamation was an illusion in which "we show our sympathy with the slaves by emancipating the slaves where we cannot reach them and holding them in bondage where we can set them free."

Lincoln did not *emancipate the slaves, greatly or otherwise.*

The same points have been made with abundant documentation by twentieth-century scholars like Richard Hofstadter, who said the Proclamation "did not in fact free any slaves." Some of the biggest names in the Lincoln establishment have said the same thing. Roy P. Basler, the editor of the monumental *Collected Works of Abraham Lincoln*, said the Proclamation was "itself only a promise of freedom. . . ." J.G. Randall, who has been called "the greatest Lincoln scholar of all time," said the Proclamation itself did not free a single slave. Horace White, the *Chicago Tribune* correspondent who covered Lincoln in Illinois and in Washington, said it is doubtful that the Proclamation "freed anybody anywhere."

There, then, the secret is out! The most famous act in American political history never happened.

[Carl] Sandburg wrote tens of thousands of words about it.

[Vachel] Lindsay wrote a poem about it.

[Aaron] Copland wrote a musical portrait about it.

[Martin Luther] King had a dream about it.

But the awkward fact is that Abraham Lincoln didn't do it. To paraphrase what Robert McColley said about the abortive emancipating initiative of Thomas Jefferson, never did man achieve more fame for what he did not do *and for what he never intended to do.* The best authority, Lincoln himself, told one of his top aides that he knew that the Proclamation in and of itself would not "make a single Negro free beyond our military reach," thereby proving two critical and conclusive points. The first is that Lincoln himself knew that his most famous act would not of itself free a single Negro. The second and most damaging point is that "the great emancipator" did not intend for it to free a single Negro, for he carefully, deliberately, studiously excluded all Negroes *within* "our military reach."

In what some critics call a hoax and others call a ploy not to free African-Americans but to keep them in slavery, Lincoln deliberately drafted the Proclamation so that it wouldn't free a single slave immediately.

What Lincoln did—and it was so clever that we ought to stop calling him honest Abe—was to "free" slaves in Confederate-held territory where he couldn't free them and to leave them in slavery in Union-held territory where he could have freed them. . . .

A growing body of evidence suggests that Lincoln's Proclamation was a tactical move designed not to emancipate the slaves but to keep as many slaves as possible in slavery until Lincoln could mobilize support for his conservative plan to free Blacks gradually and to ship them out of the country. What Lincoln was trying to do, then, from our standpoint, was to outmaneuver the real emancipators and to contain the emancipation tide, which had reached such a dangerous intensity that it threatened his ability to govern and to run the war machinery.

This is no mere theory; there is indisputable evidence on this point in documents and in the testimony of reliable witnesses, including Lincoln himself. The most telling testimony comes not from twentieth-century critics but from cronies and confidants who visited the White House and heard the words from Lincoln's mouth. There is, for example, the testimony of Judge David Davis, the three-hundred-plus-pound Lincoln crony who visited the White House in 1862, some two months after Lincoln signed the Preliminary Proclamation, and found him working feverishly to subvert his *announced* plan in favor of his *real* plan. What was Lincoln's real plan? It was the only emancipation plan he ever had: gradual emancipation, the slower the better, with compensation to slaveowners and the deportation of the emancipated. His "whole soul," Davis said, "is absorbed in *his* plan [my italics] of remunerative emancipation, and he thinks that if Congress don't fail him, that the problem is solved. . . ."

Wait a minute! What's going on here? *What* plan of remunerative emancipation? Two months ago, Abraham Lincoln announced to the whole world that he was going to free the slaves of rebels with a stroke of the pen on January 1. He didn't say anything then about Congress not letting him down.

What are we to understand by all this? We are to understand, among other things, that words, especially Lincoln's words, are deceiving and that Lincoln announced his first plan as a mask to cover his real plan and his real end. That at any rate is the testimony of another intimate Lincoln friend, Henry Clay Whitney. What was his real end? The Proclamation, Whitney said, was "not the end designed by him, but only the *means* to the end, the end being the deportation of the slaves and the payment for them to their masters—at least to those who were loyal."

Lincoln was trying . . . to outmaneuver the real emancipators and to contain the emancipation tide.

There is corroboration on this point from, of all people, Abraham Lincoln, who asked Congress in his second State of the Union Message to approve not the Emancipation Proclamation but an entirely different plan, the real plan he had confided to Judge Davis, a plan that contradicted the Proclamation and called for, among other things, the *deportation*—his word—of Blacks and the racial cleansing of the United States of America. . . .

Lincoln knew what he was doing. Not only that, he told everybody what he was doing, and everybody, or almost everybody, has refused to read and understand the words he wrote to describe what he was doing. In both the Preliminary Proclamation, and in a quotation in the final Proclamation, Lincoln said in the same sentence that the slaves in designated areas would be free and that the government would do nothing to repress them "in any efforts they may make for their actual freedom."

Actual: this is the word that gives the game away. Lincoln said he was giving the slaves freedom, and that the government would not repress them if they decided to run away and *actually* free themselves. Of such nuances of language are Memorials on the Mall made.

In his use of language and in his skill in using words to conceal and confuse, Abraham Lincoln resembles Booker T. Washington more than any other American leader, and it is fascinating—and depressing—to watch him playing with the yawning chasm between the show freedom of the Proclamation and "actual" freedom. He even proposed a constitutional amendment to pay "loyal" "owners" of "slaves who shall have enjoyed *actual* freedom by the chances of the war."

This language provides irrefutable proof that Abraham Lincoln never intended to provide for the actual freedom of the slaves, and it is embarrassing to have to say what almost everybody overlooks, and that is that *the most famous document on slavery in history does not deal with slavery at all, does not in fact use the word* slavery *at all,* pretending, in language any first-year law student could have ripped to shreds, to free certain vaguely defined slaves.

If African-Americans had relied on that document alone, they would still be in slavery in several states and areas. The Proclamation didn't apply to the Border States and Tennessee, and it excepted, as we have seen, certain slaves, a lot of slaves, in other states. If we were relying on the Emancipation Proclamation today, then, Blacks would still be in slavery in Delaware, Kentucky, Maryland, Missouri, Tennessee, part of Virginia and part of Louisiana.

What about the slaves in other areas? Would they be free?

Probably not, for the Proclamation, as Lincoln pointed out to anybody who would listen, was a war document of limited legality and scope, and its writ would probably have ended, as Lincoln said, with the end of the war. Worse, there were so many legal loopholes in the document itself that, standing alone, it would have triggered at least a century of litigation. . . .

Lincoln didn't free the slaves. If it had been left up to him, Blacks would have remained in slavery to 1900 or even longer. In a September 1858 speech, he said, "I do not suppose that in the most peaceful way ultimate extinction [of slavery] would occur in less than a hundred years at the least," which would have pushed emancipation to September 1958 "at least," twenty-nine years after the birth of Martin Luther King Jr. and four years after *Brown* v. *Board of Education*. If Lincoln had had his way, Oprah Winfrey, Martin Luther King Jr., Jesse Jackson Sr., Lena Horne, Booker T. Washington, Thurgood Marshall, Duke Ellington, Muhammad Ali, Jesse Owens, Louis Armstrong, W.C. Handy, Hank Aaron, Maya Angelou, Debbie Allen, Benjamin Quarles, Josephine Baker, Mary McLeod Bethune, Ralph Bunche, Malcolm X, Rosa Parks, Leontyne Price, Bessie Smith, Walter White, Madame C.J. Walker, Maxine Waters, Count Basie, Gwendolyn Brooks, Ida B. Wells-Barnett, Richard Wright, Alex Haley, and even Clarence Thomas would have been born in slavery.

Chronology

1820

The Missouri Compromise passes Congress. In addition to jointly admitting Missouri as a slave state and Maine as a free state, the law forbids slavery in all Louisiana Purchase lands north of 36°30' (except Missouri).

1850

Senator Henry Clay launches the Senate debate on what will become the Compromise of 1850. The bill passes and is signed into law by President Millard Fillmore. Among the bill's provisions, the slave trade is abolished in Washington, D.C., and a new, more restrictive Fugitive Slave Law is enacted, with heavy penalties for those who interfere with the capture and return of escaped slaves. California is admitted to the Union as a free state; New Mexico and Utah are admitted as territories, with the power to decide on their own whether to permit slavery (a doctrine known as popular sovereignty).

1854

The Kansas-Nebraska Act is passed in Congress, voiding the 1820 Missouri Compromise and potentially extending slavery into territories north of 36°30' under the doctrine of popular sovereignty. The act is published by Senator Stephen A. Douglas of Illinois; it is supported by southern senators and congressmen but is bitterly opposed by northerners.

1855–1856

The Kansas territory becomes a political and military battleground over the issue of slavery's expansion. Both "slave" and "free" factions seek recognition from Washington.

1857

The Supreme Court decision of *Dred Scott v. Sandford* is announced. The Court rules that blacks are not citizens and therefore cannot bring suit in federal courts; that since slaves are property, they may be taken anywhere in the United

States without losing their slave status; and that the Missouri Compromise establishing a border between slave and free territory was unconstitutional.

1858
Illinois senator Stephen Douglas and Republican nominee Abraham Lincoln engage in a series of debates on slavery and race relations as they vie for Douglas's Senate seat.

1860
Abraham Lincoln wins the Republican presidential nomination. The Republican platform opposes slavery in the territories and supports the admission of Kansas as a free state. Lincoln is elected president of the United States.

December 20, 1860
South Carolina becomes the first state to secede from the Union.

January 9, 1861
Mississippi secedes from the Union.

January 10–February 1, 1861
Florida, Alabama, Georgia, Louisiana, and Texas secede.

February–March 1861
Delegates from the seven seceded states meet in Montgomery, Alabama, to form the Confederate States of America. Jefferson Davis is inaugurated as the Confederate president.

March 4, 1861
Lincoln is inaugurated as the sixteenth president of the United States.

September 22, 1862
Lincoln issues a preliminary proclamation.

January 1, 1863
The Emancipation Proclamation takes effect. The proclamation in its final form lays more emphasis on the enlisting of black soldiers; by late spring, recruiting is under way throughout the North and Union-occupied areas in the South.

May 1–4, 1863
In a brilliant display of military tactics, Confederate general Robert E. Lee defeats a larger Union force in the Battle of Chancellorsville.

June 7, 1864
Lincoln is renominated for president by the Republican Party; Andrew Johnson, a Tennessee Democrat who remained loyal to the Union, is named his running mate.

November 8, 1864
Lincoln is reelected, carrying all but three states.

January 31, 1865
Congress approves the Thirteenth Amendment to the Constitution, which abolishes slavery.

April 9, 1865
Lee surrenders to Grant at Appomattox Courthouse.

April 14, 1865
Lincoln is assassinated by John Wilkes Booth, a Confederate sympathizer; Andrew Johnson assumes the presidency.

December 13, 1865
The Thirteenth Amendment to the Constitution is ratified by the states.

For Further Research

Books

George Anastaplo, "The Emancipation Proclamation," in *Abraham Lincoln: A Constitutional Biography*. New York: Rowman & Littlefield, 1999.

Paul M. Angle, *Created Equal? The Complete Lincoln-Douglas Debates of 1858*. Chicago: The University of Chicago Press, 1958.

Roy P. Basler, ed., *Abraham Lincoln: His Speeches and Writings*. New York: World, 1946.

———, *The Collected Works of Abraham Lincoln*. New Brunswick, NJ: Rutgers University Press, 1953.

Charles A. Beard and Mary R. Beard, *The Rise of American Civilization*. New York: Macmillan, 1927.

Ira Berlin, *Slaves No More: Three Essays on Emancipation and the Civil War*. London: Cambridge University Press, 1992.

Henry C. Clay, *Life and Speeches of Henry Clay, Vol II*. Boston: Samuel N. Dickinson, 1843.

William C. Davis, ed., *A Fire-Eater Remembers: The Confederate Memoir of Robert Barnwell Rhett*. Columbia: University of South Carolina Press, 2000.

George Fitzburgh, "Sociology for the South," in *Slavery Defended: The Views of the Old South*, ed. Eric L. McKitrick. New Jersey: Prentice-Hall, 1963.

John Hope Franklin, *The Emancipation Proclamation*. Wheeling, Illinois: Harlan Davidson, 1995.

Robert A. Goldwin, ed., *100 years of Emancipation*. Chicago: Rand McNally, 1969.

Howard Jones, *Abraham Lincoln and a New Birth of Freedom*. Lincoln: University of Nebraska Press, 1999.

William K. Klingaman, *Abraham Lincoln and the Road to Emancipation, 1861–1865*. New York: Viking Penguin, 2001.

Roger L. Ransom, *Conflict and Compromise: The Political Economy of Slavery, Emancipation, and the American Civil War.* New York: Cambridge University Press, 1989.

Wiley Sword, *Southern Invincibility: A History of the Confederate Heart.* New York: St. Martin's Press, 1999.

Hans L. Trefousse, *Lincoln's Decision for Emancipation.* New York: J.B. Lippincott, 1975.

———, *The Radical Republicans*, New York: Alfred A. Knopf, 1969.

Justin G. Turner, *The Thirteenth Amendment and the Emancipation Proclamation.* Los Angeles: Plantin Press, 1971.

Index